Book 1

Learn From Masters

Mastering The Art of Selling Anything

Mike Mohebbi

I Publish My Ideas And Findings On My Blog:

http://www.passivecashflowacademy.com

And My Facebook Page:

http://www.facebook.com/PassvieCashflowAcademy

Table Of Content

Introduction

I firmly believe that mastering the Art Of Selling is the ultimate power that we, Entrepreneurs, Must learn and master. When I found out that I need this skill and I knew nothing about it, I started searching to find good sources and materials to learn this skill.

Chapter 1: Main Challenge of a Salesman

In any type of business, big or small, new or old, there are some days that things don't go the way you plan. Orders don't deliver on time, some workers are sick and the entire production rate drops, a new competitor takes away a big chunk of your market etc. In these hard times if somebody asks you: " How's Business?", you don't want to tell them that business is terrible. Saying that you feel you've reached the end of the world actually makes a lot of people happy, especially those who are jealous of your success or are your competitors. But you can do one thing, and that is get excited and say: "Unbelievable!" It covers what you mean either way, don't you think? I've done it, it works like charm.

Everybody is in the profession of selling, one way or another. Children, spouses ... In the selling profession, the medium we use are strategies, techniques and questioning skills, when we paint the picture for the buyer properly, the positive emotions of them to say "Yes" to your offering is created. The biggest challenge that most of the sales people have is that when they start selling, they may not understand why nobody says "Yes" logically. The buyers say "Yes" emotionally, then they defend that decision logically. So, my advice for all of you sales people no matter what you sell is : "Always Remember, if you are in the business of moving people into Yes, decisions are made primarily emotionally".

The first thing that you as a salesman must do, before you want to be successful, is investing in yourself with getting proper education. Anybody who wants to master the art of selling, must find some related courses and attends seminars and reads books about sales. As a true salesman, you must search for pearls in the education programs. The certain things that can change your life and you apply them into your life. *This is the real key.*

Most of the people think that to be a salesman, you should be a good talker. The first key to success in sales is "You must buy what you sell", If you want to have true integrity. You must believe in what you do. You must get involved in your product. People will say "Yes" more to your belief and conviction than to your technical skills.

Chapter 2: **Top 3 Things to Mastering the Art of Selling Anything**

To Master the Art of Selling Anything, There are three things that you must have first:

1. You must find a product that you so believe in that you are excited about it.
2. You need to find qualified people to sell and sell professionally to them by using your sales skills to lead them to say "Yes".
3. You have to help people to make decisions that are GOOD FOR THEM.

There is a basic truth that all the salespeople have to live by in the field of sales. It says: " If I Say It, They Tend To doubt It. If They say it, It's True". The key is to take any statement of fact and see how you can turn it into a question. There are some questions that you must master and you can apply them to all areas of your life.

If you want to be passionate about what you sell, you must be careful what to choose for selling. Many sales people don't care about this crucial step and think that if you are a good salesman, you must be able to sell anything. Well, that's partially true. You can sell anything, but sometimes you lose your momentum and desire to sell, especially when the sales rate goes down the hill. If you are not passionate about what you sell, there's a high chance that you quit selling that product, even if it could be a gem in the trash.

Finding qualified people to sell to is a skill that you will learn over time. When you put effort into the business and see all types of potential buyers, you will get a sense of who the true buyer is and who is not. Developing this skill is not theoretical and must be practiced, so you must talk to many people and try to find the desire to buy your product in their words. Then you can get to high rate of success by utilizing a good sales pitch process.

You must always have this idea before your mind that you want to help people to solve their problems. If you can do this truly and transfer this helping feeling to people, it's then that they become lifelong buyers. How many times have you bought something that you find out it's useless and a piece of junk after you take it home, and you thought: "I'll never buy from that seller ever". Your true job is to help others finding what they want easier and through this process you can cash in a lot of profit.

Chapter 3: **Critical Questions For a Salesman**

Bonding Question: It's a question at the end of a sentence that demands a "YES" response.

- I said it, *didn't I?*
- that's true, *isn't it?*
- You're catching on. *aren't you?*
- They're very beautiful, *aren't they?*

The rule for the Bonding Question is that it shouldn't be overused. The major rule is for every hour of presentation, there shouldn't be more than two bonding questions in the presentation. If you use more than twice in your speech, you seem like pushy and people won't buy from you.

Alternate of Choice: It's a question with two answers. The trick here is that either answer the client chooses is a minor agreement towards the major decision. You must always try to give them two questions. The key is that they *must* know the answer. This is very important. The answer must confirm the fact that they are going ahead.

The best way you can use this question is:

- Time to meet someone. Use their name and say: " Mike, I'm available to meet you today at 3:00 or tomorrow at 9:00. Now, they can't say yes or no. They should take 3 or 9, either way you have to meet with them.
- You can use it on locations. "Would you come to my facility or should I come to your home?". They can't say yes or no. They have to take a place, home or office.

My daughter knows how to use this question. Instead of asking for permission to play with computer, she asks: " dad! which one do you prefer me to do? Watch TV or play Minecraft?" either way, she gets what she wants.

You can use it on your spouse. You know you have nothing in the house, you just smile and say: " What would you like tonight honey? Chinese or Italian food?" Either way, you will be out for dinner. How's that? ;)

Magic Mirror: I call this question Magic Mirror because it's easy to forget and the name of magic mirror helps your brain to remember it easily. It's answering the right question with a right question and write that answer on you paperwork. You turn the buyer's question back to them by asking another question.

- If they ask: "How soon can you deliver ...?" You must ask back: "Mike, what time schedule will best suit you?" When they answer that, in essence, you close the sale.
- "Do you have a Japanese brand?" you ask back:" Do you like a Japanese brand?", By saying YES, you close the transaction.
- "Do you have a smaller size?" you ask back:" would you like a smaller size?" and again by saying YES, you close the transaction.

When the say "YES", the have bought. So simple.

Chapter 4: Why Don't People Buy Your Product When They Should?

There are ten reasons why people don't buy your products. These ten fears are the cause of that a human being has to invest his/her money for the benefit of a product. If you want to increase your sales rate, you must know these fears and you must work on them. You must work on your presentation so that it smartly eliminates these ten fears. The reason these fears exist is because people know you are a salesman and they know what you do for living (*Selling your product*). Here are the ten fears:

They are afraid of you! Because they are afraid to be sold. People are great consumers, they love to own things but, people nowadays are afraid to be sold. The key is not to show yourself as a salesperson but an "Expert Advisor". When you do this, they stop looking at you as a person who wants to sell them. They must love you, trust you and want to listen to you. This is the key factor in selling anything to anyone. If this happens and they trust you, they want more information and it's then your time to show them your sales skills.

They are afraid of making a mistake! Many people have purchased something that they wish they had never purchased or they have been told something that it didn't work or the warranty was not good so, they have this fear that they don't want to make that mistake again. It is your duty to watch closely the presentation to cover all those mistakes.

They are afraid of being lied to! Almost all the people above 30 years of age have purchased something where it didn't do what it was said it was going to do and they felt they were lied to. That's why you should be extremely honest and truthful. You must have a long term integrity and ethics with your clients.

They are afraid of incurring debt! So many people have too much debt today and when they look at your product, they think they can't afford it. So, again, it's your responsibility to show them the value they get. This is the true meaning of selling, to exchange information and value with cost and money. It starts with perceived value as to the benefit they are going to get. Then from perceived value it goes to real value. Here the key is learning how to pour on value. if there is enough value it diminishes the investment they are going to make.

The fear of losing face! This fear is more obvious when you are selling something to a couple. If you threaten the ego and face of one of them in front of the other one, they won't buy anything from you. The key here is to make everybody at the table feel important. Never talk down to anybody, never belittle anyone. When you make everybody feel important, you actually uplift them and they do business with you not once but, for a lifetime. That's the ultimate sale's goal, to make somebody a lifetime client. (*It's good to know that in the last year of being in sales, 96% of Tom Hopkins' customers were referred to him from a happy client*). This only happens when they find out that you care more about them than making a sale. In other words, you must have empathy for them. Empathy is putting yourself in their shoes.

They are afraid of unknown! They are afraid of the product they know nothing about. It's your job to make the presentation an educational process. You must show them the benefits of your product for them.

They have the fear of bad past experience! If you sound like the person who sold them a bad thing last time, they have the feeling that " I've had that bad experience before. I won't buy from you again". You should be careful with people about their bad past purchase experiences, especially with people over fifty years of age. You must give them the feeling of security and trust until they think that your product is really good for them.

Two fears together, Their fears can be based on prejudice and it is based on the third party. You must be careful about the customers who Someone has prejudiced them. Their parents said they shouldn't do it, their grandparents said they shouldn't do it, they are prejudiced by the third party and now they are afraid of making a mistake and then being blamed by that third party. **This fear of being criticized overwhelms them and they cannot go ahead.**

They have the fear of the words you say! When you are in the art of selling, you use words to paint a beautiful picture for the customer's ear, just like a painter who uses different oils to make the painting more and more beautiful and attractive to the eye. You must be careful with the words you say and every word you say has one of these two effects on people; either it's a positive effect or a negative effect. There are eight words that you must never use under any circumstances.

Chapter 5: **The Eight Forbidden Words That a Salesman Must Never Use**

A person can be very close to say "yes" or very close to say "no" and when they hear one of these eight words, the fear overwhelms them.

First Word Is *Cost*!

When you want to tell them how much your product or your service is, you shall never use the words "COST" or "PRICE". Because as soon as you say "the cost is..." or "the price is...", their first reaction is "it's too much" or " we should shop around for a better price". So, you must never use these two words, instead you can use "Total Investment" or "Total Amount".

The second word is *Down Payment!*

The first thing people think about when they hear this word is "God, I didn't even think that I have to come up with any money right now". For them, the word down payment means writing a cheque and the first think they think about is " We're not doing that, we're just looking today, we're just shopping, we're not buying today" and then they go to the dealer round the corner. So, instead of using "Down Payment" use "Initial Investment" or "Initial Amount". These words do not create the fear that the down payment creates.

The third word is *Monthly Payment!*

When you say monthly payment, it takes them back to that monthly sitting around the kitchen table to calculate the bills and payments and the hope that they have enough money in their bank account to pay the bills. It scares them. So never ever use the word "monthly payment" instead use "Monthly Investment" or "Monthly Amount".

Never call it a *Contract!*

When you say "let's go to the contract" they remember their mum and dad saying "Don't you get near a contract, either you must read all the little prints and if you don't understand it, make sure you get an attorney involved". All that is built in their memory and when you use the word "contract" they remember that saying. So, instead of using "contract" use either "The Paperwork" or "The Agreement" or "The Form". Can you see the whole different feeling these words have?

Don't say the word *Buy!*

When you say "You buy this" that's what they don't want to do, they're there to look. Instead of using the word "Buy" use the word "Own". People love to own things, they are only afraid to buy them and the feeling and proud of ownership gives them power and security. You actually help them emotionally say "Yes".

The next two words are *Sell* and *Sold!*

When you tell people "I'm selling you this" suddenly they say " you're not doing that, we decided we're not buying and you're not selling anything to us". Or when some salespeople say "you know, we sold your friend as well", and the think "yah! you pushed them into it. You're not doing that to me". So drop the word "Sell" or "Sold", instead use the words "Get Them Involved" or "Help Them Acquire". Say "We've helped so many......acquire this......". It's very amazing that people let you get them involved or they let you help them acquired, they just don't want you t sell them.

Never use the word *Deal!*

So many people have gotten into a bad deal that they had been told it was a good deal. So when you say "It's a good deal" they go back and think " we had one of those, no thank you, we're not getting involved in another deal". Specially people over fifty remember losing all of their savings in a deal that somebody told them it was a good deal and it wasn't. So, instead of using "Deal" use "Opportunity" or "Transaction".

Now, you're doing everything right, you've filled out the paperwork and it's time to go for the signature.

Never ask them to *Sign* it!

Do not ask people to sign anything. When they are heading towards a "Yes", by only using this word, you can push them into "No". They remember their mum and dad saying "Don't you sign anything!". So, instead of word "Sign" you can ask them "Mr. ..... I just need you to OK it here" or you can ask them to "Approve" it or ask them to "Authorize" it or even you can ask them to "Endorse" it, but never ask them to sign it. It's very amazing that they Ok it, they Approve it, they Authorize it, they Endorse it but they hardly Sign it. It's amazing to know that when you ask them to sign it, they say " we're going to think it over, we'll get back to you".

When you ask them "John, I need you to sign my paperwork here and we set the delivery for the next week", some of them don't know what you mean. That's why many of them ask "Oh! you mean you want us to sign it" and you must give them a nice smile, nod your head and just say one word "Fine" and now they know what their job is.

Here we come to the artwork of the art of selling and it's **Closing The Sale.** This is the one area that people have the most challenge with. Most of the salespeople can prospect, they can make calls, they can do a decent presentation but where they fall down is moving from "Giving Information and Sharing All the Presentation" to "The Final Closing The Sale". Closing a sale successfully is an art form, many blow it up in the last second. This is the art that you want to fully master. This is the one thing that you cannot copy from anybody. You can listen, watch and learn from many sales masters but you must _develop your own style._

Chapter 6: **Definition of Closing**

Closing is professionally using a person's desire to own the benefits of your product, then blending your sincere desire to serve in helping the person making the decision that's truly _good for them._ When you close a sale, you are actually doing four things:

1.   You help the clients rationalize the decision they want to make.
2.   You help clients head off procrastination.
3.   You help clients deal with their fear.
4.   You help clients overcome indecision.

The Final Closing begins in one of these three ways:

1.   Buyer asks you a porcupine question. You write down the answer of that question on the paper work bu saying "Let me make a note of that". If they ask "Tom, would you train us to use the copier?" you don't say "Yes", you'd smile and say" is training the thing you like?" if they say "Yes", you reach for the

paperwork work, say "Let me make a note of that" and write "Training required" and that closes the sale.

2.   You ask them the final closing question. It's a minor or a test close. You ask them "John, how are you feeling about all of this so far?" You didn't ask them to but, you only asked about their feeling and when they say " i'm feeling good", it's time to move to the paperwork by saying "let me make a note of that".

3.   You ask them a reflex question and move on to your paperwork. The most popular reflex question is the "Date". Just smile and say "you know John, I've been running in such a paste, do you know the date?", first you show that you are well off because you don't know the date and when he gives you the answer, you thank him and put it down on the paperwork and you're closing. Second question is "The Correct Spelling of The name". If their name is hard to pronounce, you may ask them " Mr. .... can you help me with your name?" and as he spells it, you fill it out on the form. The third one is "Asking For Their Initials". "Marry! did you have a middle initial?", she says yes and you say " let me make a note of that" and you're closing the deal.

When everything is done and you've finished filling out the form, pick it up and scan it for correctness and deliver your final closing sentence; "John, with your approval right here, we set up the delivery for the next week". This is a sample sentence and you can develop your own.

Important Note: Whenever you   ask   the final question,   you must _shut up!_ you can't imagine how many deals never close just because the salesman talks after the last question and they end up owning the product. Let the customer have it. You just sit back and let them sign the paperwork for you.

Chapter 7: How To Handle The Word "I Want To Think It Over

When you get in the business of sales, you will hear the word "I want to think it over" many times. You must know what to say. This is one of the important skills you must learn in your career as a salesman. Whenever you hear this sentence, you must smile and say "Oh! that's fine John. Obviously you wouldn't take your time thinking this thing over unless you were seriously interested, would you? I mean I'm sure you're not telling me that to get rid of me , I assume". He will agree. then you must say "Just to clarify my thinking, what phase of this opportunity you like to think it over? Is it the quality of the service I render? Is it the color? Is it something I forgot to cover?". She says "No" to all of that and then you simply say "Seriously, tell me could it be the money?"

 Because nine out of ten times it is money. He will probably say: "I think it costs too much!". Now you just smile and say "You know, today most things do, can you tell me how much you feel is too much?". And you will get an amount of money. You can now move to the next strategy which is called "The Reduction To The Ridiculous!". You must take the amount of money, find the number of years they're going to enjoy the product, get it to an annual amount, then go to the monthly, then weekly and then to the daily amount. In this way, a home can cost 35 cents a day instead of costing 3200$ extra that they wanted to pay for the period of thirty years. This Reduction To Ridiculous is a fabulous technique.

Chpter8: **Psychology And Power Of Affirmations**

You got to learn to have a positive attitude every day in your business. There is no successful salesman who is successful without getting some adrenalin pumping". Here is what I think a good routine and it must be done three times a day with enthusiasm:

1. I always call my best prospects first.

2. I am in a positive attitude towards myself, my selling profession and my prospects.

3. I always help my clients to find the best they want.

4. I am a disciplined salesman.

5. I always follow my sales presentation step by step.

6. I improve my ability to listen and learn every day.

Do this and get that excitement and joy running into your blood, and get out excited for the day. Have a greater income and be the person of your dreams.

Wish you good luck!

I publish my ideas and findings on my blog at:

http://www.PassiveCashflowAcademy.com

and my Facebook page at:

https://www.facebook.com/PassvieCashflowAcademy

www.ingramcontent.com/pod-product-compliance
Lightning Source LLC
Chambersburg PA
CBHW061239180526
45170CB00003B/1364